What Makes a Family?

Diana Kenney, M.A.Ed., NBCT

Consultants

Shelley Scudder
Gifted Education Teacher
Broward County Schools

Caryn Williams, M.S.Ed.
Madison County Schools
Huntsville, AL

Publishing Credits

Dona Herweck Rice, *Editor-in-Chief*
Lee Aucoin, *Creative Director*
Torrey Maloof, *Editor*
Diana Kenney, M.A.Ed., NBCT, *Associate Education Editor*
Marissa Rodriguez, *Designer*
Stephanie Reid, *Photo Editor*
Rachelle Cracchiolo, M.S.Ed., Publisher

Image Credits: Cover & p. 1 Shutterstock; Back Cover Diana Kenney; p. 20 Alamy; p. 8 (right) Diana Kenney; p. 7 (top) Maribel Rendon; pp. 12, 15, 17, 21 Getty Images; p. 8 (left) The Granger Collection, New York; p.7(bottom) iStockphoto; p. 4 The Library of Congress [LC-USW3-016694-C]; p. 14 The Library of Congress [LC-USZ62-123735]; p. 16 The Library of Congress [LC-USF34-056964-D]; p. 18 The Library of Congress [LC-DIG-ppmsca-09452]; p. 24 The Library of Congress [LC-USF34-056964-D]; p. 6 Joey Rice; pp. 19 ThinkStock; All other images from Shutterstock.

Teacher Created Materials
5301 Oceanus Drive
Huntington Beach, CA 92649-1030
http://www.tcmpub.com

ISBN 978-1-4333-6970-4

Printed by: 51497
Printed in: China

Table of Contents

Families

Families are great! They may not all look the same. But the people all love one another.

This is a family picture from 1942.

All Sizes

Some families are big.
They have lots of people.
Other families are small.

This is a family picture from today.

A Shared Past

Every family has a past. Photos help tell about the past. Drawings and stories help, too.

This drawing tells about a wedding.

The First Photo

The first color photo was taken in 1861.

Color pictures get better every year.

Objects also tell about a family. They tell about parts of the family's life. They help us learn about the past.

Many people keep baby books and special toys.

A Piece of History

An **heirloom** (AIR-loom) is an object. A family owns it for many years. It is passed down in a family from older people to younger people.

A pocket watch or a necklace can be an heirloom.

A Shared Culture

Every family has a **culture**. *Culture* is the way people think and live. It includes **traditions** (truh-DISH-uhnz), or things they do all the time.

Diwali is a Hindu tradition. It is the Festival of Lights.

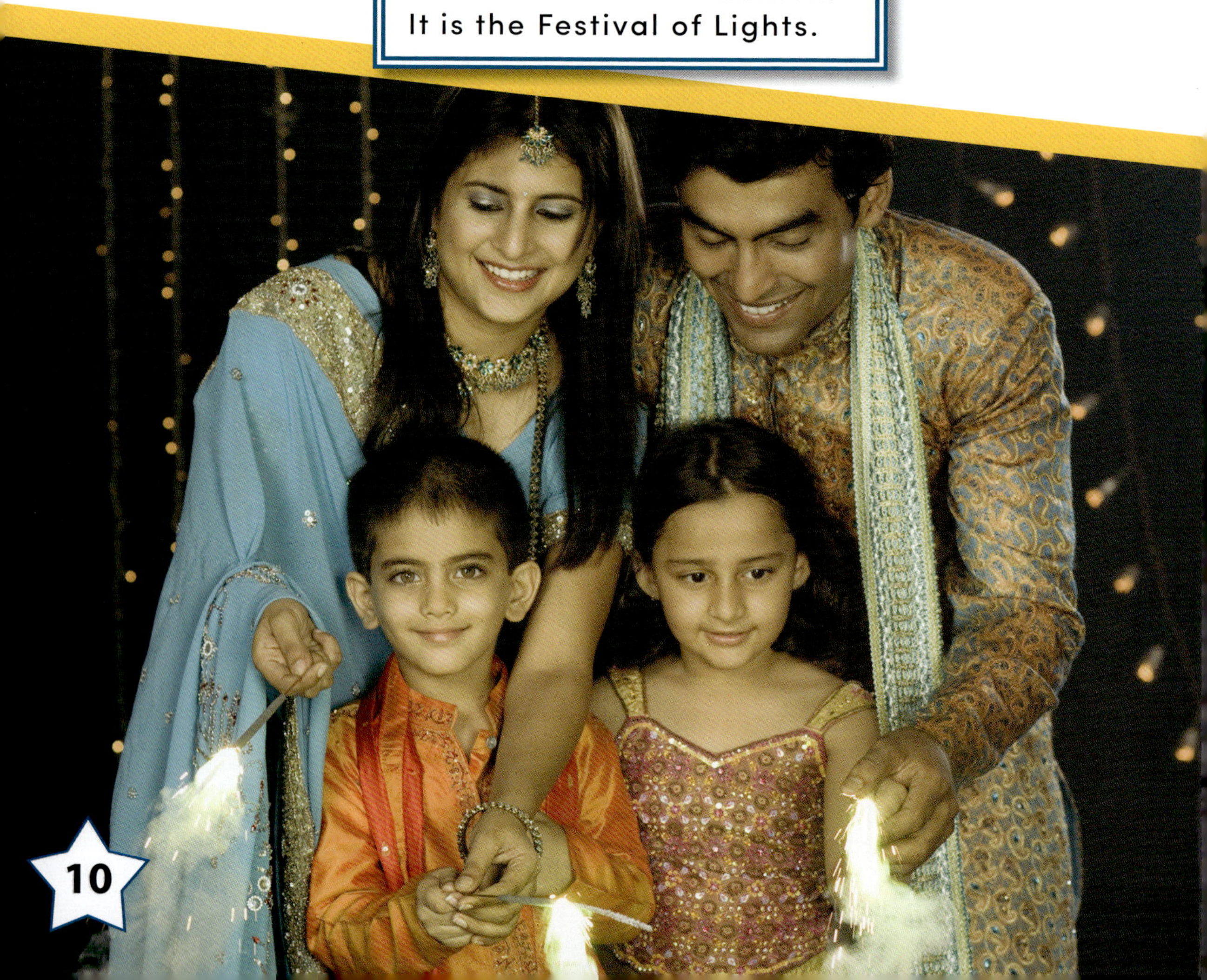

Take off Your Shoes

In some cultures, families take off their shoes before going into a home. This helps keep the home clean.

Time to Celebrate

A **celebration** (sel-uh-BREY-shuhn) is a party. Families have many celebrations. They may celebrate **holidays**. They may celebrate one another.

A family celebrates a birthday in 1949.

A family celebrates a birthday today.

Time to Share

Every family shares. They share **responsibilities** (ri-spon-suh-BIL-i-teez). They take care of one another.

A girl helps her mother wash clothes in 1870.

A boy helps his dad wash clothes today.

Families also share time. They eat meals together. They go on trips. They have fun.

This family has a picnic at the beach in 1941.

Road Trips

Some families go on long trips in their cars. These are called *road trips*.

This family takes a road trip today.

Families Are Fun!

Families are fun. They share a past. They work together. They love one another.

A family poses for a picture in 1958.

This family shares a fun day at the park.

Play It!

Plan a family game night. Choose a game you like to play and tell your family members the rules. Have them teach you games they like to play. Have a fun night as a family!

This family plays a board game long ago.

This family plays a board game today.

Glossary

celebration—a party for a special day

culture—the way people think and live

heirloom—an object that is passed down in a family from older people to younger people

holidays—special days to celebrate

responsibilities—jobs you have to do

traditions—ways of doing things all the time

Index

Your Turn!

My Family

All families are special! This is a photo of a family long ago. How is your family the same? How is it different?